GARDEN
PROVERBS

GARDEN PROVERBS

"IF YOU WOULD BE HAPPY
ALL YOUR LIFE—
PLANT A GARDEN."

Collected and Edited by Terry Berger

RUNNING PRESS
PHILADELPHIA · LONDON

Library of Congress Cataloging-in-Publication Number
93–85530

ISBN 1-56138-358-9

This book may be ordered by mail from the publisher.
Please add $1.00 for postage and handling.
But try your bookstore first!
Running Press Book Publishers
125 South Twenty-second Street
Philadelphia, Pennsylvania 19103-4399

CONTENTS

*S*ome years ago, my father offered me the following advice: "Love is not like a potato. You can't throw it out the window."

He was right.

Soon I was wondering if there were proverbs about carrots, peas, and corn. Before long, I had collected a bushelful of proverbs about fruits and vegetables and flowers and how to plant and care for them. Gathering the best, I lovingly planted them in this little book.

These proverbs give practical advice to gardeners, and at the same time nourish their spirits—for the garden is a metaphor for life itself. Although not all of us are gardeners, we all plant the seeds of family and friendship. And yes, we must carefully tend them to make them grow. To everyone who is part of the cycle of life, the wisdom in this book offers a bountiful harvest of inspiration.

THE EARTH

One generation
passeth away,
and another gen-
eration cometh;
but the earth
abideth forever.

THE OLD TESTAMENT,
ECCLESIASTES 1:4

10 GARDEN PROVERBS

The poetry of the earth
is never dead.

JOHN KEATS

Speak to the earth,
and it shall
teach thee.

THE OLD TESTAMENT,
JOB 12:8

Until you approach
a deep ravine
you do not realize the
thickness of
the earth.

CHINESE

The earth laughs
at him who calls a place
his own.

HINDUSTANI

The earth is man's
only friend.

BULGARIAN

If man cheats
the earth,
the earth will
cheat man.

CHINESE

However high
a bird may soar,
it seeks its food
on earth.

DANISH

THE
SEASONS

Everything is good
in its season.

ITALIAN

Snowy winter,
a plentiful harvest.

It is not spring
'til you can plant
your foot upon
twelve daisies.

The spring is not
always green.

If you sing
all summer,
you'll weep
in winter.

If the summer
gave nothing,
neither will
the autumn.

BULGARIAN

All autumns
do not fill
granaries.

ESTONIAN

The winter
does not go
without looking
backward.

FINNISH

RAIN OR SHINE

Rain in spring
is as precious
as oil.

CHINESE

Not all clouds
bring rain.

DUTCH

30 GARDEN PROVERBS

One cloud is enough
to eclipse all the sun.

There is no sun
without a shadow.

The sky is
not less blue
because
the blind man
does not see it.

DANISH

Every day cannot be
a feast of lanterns.

CHINESE

After great droughts
come great rains.

The sun shines
brightly after
it rains.

THE GARDEN

If you
would be happy
all your life—
plant a garden.

One should
cultivate
his garden.

VOLTAIRE

The garden
is the poor man's
apothecary.

GERMAN

More grows in the
garden than was
sown there.

ENGLISH

No garden is
without weeds.

Gardens are not
made by sitting
in the shade.

RUDYARD KIPLING

Everyone has
enough to do
in weeding
his own garden.

FLEMISH

The best place
to find God
is in a garden.
You can dig for
him there.

GEORGE BERNARD SHAW

THE GARDENER

God almighty first
planted a garden.

FRANCIS BACON

Adam was a
gardener, and God,
who made him,
sees that half of all
good gardening
is done upon
the knees.

RUDYARD KIPLING

A gardener's flirtations
should take place
outside the garden.

AFGHAN

The gardener's foot
does not spoil
the garden.

ITALIAN

The gardener's hands
are black with earth
but his loaves
are white.

ALBANIAN

As is the gardener,
such is the garden.

HEBREW

He that plants trees
loves others
besides himself.

The love of
gardening is a seed
that once sown
never dies.

GERTRUDE JEKYLL

PLANTING

The way of
cultivation
is not easy.

LATIN

He who plants a garden
plants happiness.

CHINESE

Planting

As you sow,
so will you reap.

THE NEW TESTAMENT,
GALATIANS 6:7

Sow corn in clay,
and plant vines
in sand.

SPANISH

The more furrows,
the more corn.

ENGLISH

Planting

It's little good
a-watering
last year's crop.

Let your prayers
for a good crop
be short—
and your hoeing
be long.

ALBANIAN

When the root is deep,
there is no reason
to fear the wind.

CHINESE

TOOLS

The vineyard does
not require prayers,
but a hoe.

What a man needs
in gardening is a
cast-iron back
with a hinge in it.

C.D.WARNER

He that works
without tools
is twice tired.

Handle your tools
without mittens.

BENJAMIN FRANKLIN

A bad workman
quarrels with
his tools.

ENGLISH

It is no jesting with
edged tools.

Five fingers hold
more than two
forks.

GERMAN

You can
drive out nature
with a pitchfork,
but she keeps on
coming back.

HORACE

THE VEGETABLE PATCH

Love is not
like a potato.
You can't throw it
out the window.

RUSSIAN

A melon
and a woman are
hard to know.

FRENCH

Fine words
butter no parsnips.

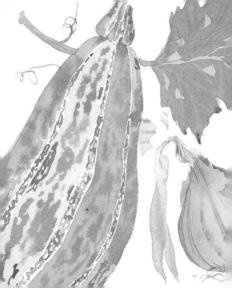

Corn can't grow
on the ceiling.

YIDDISH

There's no getting
blood out of a
turnip.

Only in dreams
are carrots as big
as bears.

YIDDISH

There grows no herb
to heal a
coward's heart.

Garlic is as good as
ten mothers.

It is bad soil
where flowers will
not grow.

The lotus springs
from the mud.

CHINESE

Every flower
has its perfume.

TURKISH

To be overcome by
the fragrance of flowers
is a delectable form of defeat.

BEVERLEY NICHOLS

The breath of flowers
is far sweeter
in the air . . .
than in the hand.

FRANCIS BACON

The rose has thorns
only for those who
would gather it.

CHINESE

Flowers beyond
reach are
sacred to God.

INDIAN

To create a
little flower
is the labor of ages.

WILLIAM BLAKE

THE ORCHARD

Fruits that
blossom first
will first be ripe.

One plum
gets color by
looking at another.

PERSIAN

The fruit should pray
for the welfare
of the leaves.

YIDDISH

If you enjoy the fruit,
pluck not the flower.

The better the fruit,
the more wasps
to eat it.

GERMAN

Go to a pear-tree
for pears—
not to an elm.

LATIN

The apple does not
fall far from the tree.

YIDDISH

Call me not olive
till you see me
gathered.

ITALIAN

HARVEST

A man must put
grain in the ground
before he can cut
the harvest.

GYPSY

The garden must be
prepared in the
soul first
or else it will not
flourish.

Tickle it with a hoe
and it will laugh
into a harvest.

ENGLISH

Pluck not
where you never
planted.

Harvest comes not
every day,
though it comes
every year.

Live within
your harvest.

He that hath a
good harvest
may be content with
some thistles.

When God blesses
the harvest,
there is enough for
the thief as well as
the gardener.

POLISH

THE FRUITS OF LABOR

That which one eats
as the fruit of his
own labor,
is properly
called food.

After stuffing pears within
drink old wine till they swim.

SPANISH

Don't make a garden
of your belly.

FRENCH

Better eat vegetables
and fear no creditors,
than eat duck and
hide from them.

THE TALMUD

Who will eat
the kernel of the nut
must break the shell.

God gives almonds
to some who
have no teeth.

SPANISH

Honey in the mouth
won't help bitterness
in the heart.

YIDDISH

All griefs
with bread are less.

This book has been bound
using handcraft methods, and
Smyth-sewn to ensure durability.

The dust jacket and interior were
designed by Nancy Loggins and
illustrated by Mary Woodin.

The text was set in Sabon with Ariston
by Richard Conklin.